Harve Mouse

by
Stuart Medland

Published by the Larks Press
Ordnance Farmhouse, Guist Bottom, Dereham
Norfolk NR20 5PF
(01328) 829207
email: Larks.Press@btinternet.com

March 2009

Printed at the Lanceni Press
Garrood Drive, Fakenham

British Library Cataloguing-in-Publication Data
A catalogue record for this book is available
from the British Library

By the same author

The Nogard
ISBN 0 948400 76 5

Return to the Nogard
ISBN 0 948400 97 8

Pinecone
ISBN 1 904 006 21 3

© Stuart Medland 2009
ISBN 978 1 904006 45 9

To

Nathan, Thomas
Abigail & Jonathan

Those Human Harvest Mice!

Contents

To Be A Harvest Mouse (or not to be)	1
SNAILshell	3
Motorfalcon	*4*
On Sheringham Beach	6
Hogweeds Have Landed	**7**
Urchins	9
Swift	**10**
New Millenium Wren	*11*
I Had A Meteorite	12
House Martians	*16*
Gingko Biloba	18
Poppyheads	**19**
Circles of Gulls	22
HORSE CHESTNUT	23
Conkers	24
wOoDcOck	26
Vasa	**29**
Sparrows Have Eroded	30
Mouse Bird	32
Nest of a Long Tailed Tit	*34*
Curlew Haiku	*35*
(The Secret World of) **Master Geoffrey's Trees**	**36**
Moorhen S t r e t c h e s	*39*
The Big Snow	40
Heights	*41*
The Highland Cow	*42*
In the Eye of the Hare	**93**
McGuffie's Toyshop	**96**
Home From School	*101*

Pantomime *with* Turnstones	45
Camel on Rails	**47**
Egret	48
Antzanaphids	49
LOOKOUT	**50**
Now He's A Customs & Excise Officer!	*52*
Beaky Billingtons	**53**
FLOAT	56
PIER	**57**
A Guillemot on Sheringham Beach	61
Owlzanbatz	*63*
Discerning the Fern	64
SAXOPHONE PLAYER	65
Don't Let Your Grandma Get Away!	66
Dental Scandal	*67*
Without My Aunty Ruth	68
Tonsils	**70**
Xmas Tonsils	**72**
Les The Barber	73
The Squirrel Man	78
At Derwentwater	*79*
STORM AT SEA	80
Sea Shrugs	88
Sleepy Flies	89
Daddy Long Legs	90
Chin-Up Stoat	**92**
Late Harvest (or, how the Cover came about!)	*102*
Sue's Teasels	**104**

Harve St Mouse **Harve St Mouse** Harve St Mouse

Welcome to Harvest Mouse! A second Rattlebag of Poems - mostly Nature Poems, some about People, a few from my Travels and a fair sprinkling of supposedly Funny ones again.

You may be wondering why I have called this book **Harvest Mouse.** Well, I'll tell you. I've called it *Harvest Mouse* because of one that I met with my daughter some years ago now, whose expression I have never forgotten. (The mouse's - not my daughter's!) He actually seemed to be curious about *me* - just for a moment - and I realised that Nature Study works both ways. *We* are being wondered about *too* - if not actually pestered and drawn and written about!

Also . . . a Harvest Mouse - if you ever had the good fortune to be introduced to one - is just the most exquisitely alive and alert, impossibly delicate-looking, tinily-charming morsel of life. It is not uncommon to fall in love with one.

A Harvest Mouse is, quite possibly, the *ideal* representative of the Natural World in its unspoken and unconscious campaign to be noticed - before it's all too late.

I hope *you enjoy my Word-Morsels too. My Poems, I mean.*
Some may be swallowed whole, almost.
Others may need chewing on a bit!

To Be A Harvest Mouse
(or not to be)

To be a Harvest Mouse

You'll need to weigh
No more than this 2p (the one
I've dropped into my hand
and I can hardly feel at all)

You'll need to be *that* small.

You'll need a tail
To hang you from a chandelier of hogweed
Or twist you, corkscrew,
Round a pogo-stick of jumpy corn . . .

The *moment* you are born.

Your fur will need to feel like thistledown
And when you're just a fortnight old
Be quite prepared to find yourself
Quite naturally . . .

Mistaken for a *bumble-bee*.

Your eyes will be
The single balls of blackberry
That make the whole one bobble-*ee*
and that your pixie hands
Can deftly spin
(just like an apple from a twig,
though not so big)
To pluck it free
From all the rest . . . *incredibly*

And roll between your knitting-needle
Fingers, letting go a curly reel of film -
A film of peel.
You'll need to be
That cool . . .

And that unreal.

SNAILshellSNAILshellSNAILshellSNAILshellSNAIL

I have a broken snail shell

Battered on a stone repeatedly
as if it was a china jug -
to pour the snail
from inside out.

Its opening (the largest part
that's left undamaged)
is a huge and empty
Speech mark or apostrophe,
that you could print
an outline of -

    with very little
    left to say.

The rest is nibbled like a crisp
around a helter-skelter apple core - a
Spiral, like a twist of gristle,
all enamelled out of snail-juice.

When I hold my snail shell
up against the daylight
I can see its darkling bands
glow terracotta - just like
strips of bacon round a
'pigs in blankets' -

Light and blow-away and
Greaseproof-paper see-through

    as a crunchy
    breakfast Cornflake.

Motorfalcon

Manages the sky
Above the motorway . . .

Has won himself a contract
for maintaining grassy banks
and verges either side -

*Six lanes to oversee
as far as the eye can see.*

Hanging from his fingertips
to suddenly let go and

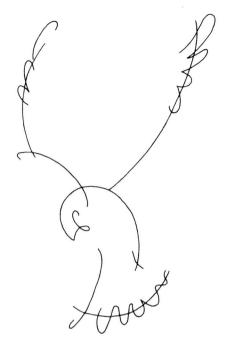

        Drop
            drop
                drop -

A grassy plop

Upon each mouse or vole or shrew
that's just about to dash into the road
and upset one more lorryload -

*Snatch it
from the
Traffic.*

Motorfalcon doesn't
need to close three lanes
for roadworks, flash his speed restrictions
at you, put up cones to redirect your
overtaking-indicating swerve -

He simply floats

Above the everlasting din -
the *need-to-be-there* speed -

And holds his nerve.

*(written in honour of the 27 kestrels I spotted
either side of the A1(M) when I went to
Scotland for my holiday last October)*

On Sheringham Beach
One Late October Afternoon

We stand at the edge of the Sea - though
it's hard to tell where that might be -

So calm, so like some water
balanced in a baking tray, and still
unspilled - its babylips
        can only bubble dribbles at us.

Half a dozen eyes keep skidding out to the horizon -
skipping side by side - and not
a single heave beneath the water
lifting it towards us - ***all this Ocean***

Barely laps, *is only rinsing
out the sand*, fingering
the little rags of seaweed
    glowing emerald
        with golding light. But

Here we are
In the lap of the milky sea
with it all run out of storms
        and big ideas - idly childish,

Mild and aimless, wanting
our attention, hardly even

swimming round our feet.

Hogweeds Have Landed!

Giant Hogweeds have landed
Up at the tip. Alien sentinels
Watching the rubbish dump.

High on their one hollow pipe of a leg
They have cranked themselves overnight
(acting the oversized weed - incognito,
standing on tiptoe - out of their
overgrown plot of allotment)

Umbellifer-ifly
Spying on human activity -
Finding, surprisingly,
All it appears to be, is

> *Throwing away*
> *By night and by day -*
> > ***Out of Mind,***
> > ***Out of sight***
> *By day and by night.*

> *Dumping it, binning it,*
> *Skipping each pile -*
> > ***Out of Sight,***
> > ***Out of mind.***
> *Home with a smile.*

Hogweeds have
Landed - banded together;

Woody umbrellas put up inside-out
Protecting their sky from our
                              rubbishy ground,
Cupping a radar-dish bowlful of
Twiggy-snap spokes to the heavens,

Raining their signals out to the stars
and begging them back again. *No-one*

Has come for them. All of their seed-saucer
Packets of saved information are lost in our
Autumn and all of their eyelashes
Bristly with looking in vain. Left

To collapse. Leaning on one, then another,
In turn. Held up by lines of bindweedy twine,
'Til, splintering, each Hogweed neck hits the deck,
Hangs its umbrella head down at the ground.

More rubbishy
Waste-ground wood
Left up at the
Throwaway dump.

Urchins

You dug me up
a sea urchin

Once, when you were
clearing tree-roots,

Thought, 'that's something
that my dad might like

Upon his desk
or somewhere' - lobbed it

Out of harm's way.
Here it is; a fossil

Cast in flint, the stripes
still visible, the glint

Where spade has clipped it
sensible of time again - miles

from any sea, passed through the
rooty fingers of a million trees

Urchin to urchin - to *you* . . .
. . . to desktop urchin *me.*

Swift

All I need is the hot June sky
for a kiln - to bake me
and break me -

*a pottery shard before
there is even a pot*

Sidestepping
all of that coming and going
To be suddenly there,

Drizzle and
Blown sand low over desert
To wet me and dry me
smooth and sharp

*Ever thrown
and ever*

Coming back.

New Millenium Wren

Celebrates
each part-moment
with a flying trill of
body-piercing decibels -

a fingernail . . .
bulleting along bright beads.

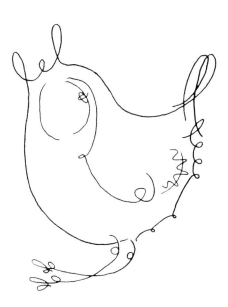

I Had A Meteorite

I had a meteorite (well, half)

- a hemisphere of polished glass,
a cricket ball that once came spinning
out of Space, a dirty giant walnut

Sliced clean through

and inside - glued together
in their tumble through the white-hot sky
(a pencil line of light that no-one saw) -
a pocketful of minerals,

A tiny mine of solar secrets
in my crusty-crystal egg.

I had an eagle's skull

that *wasn't* made of old and dirty plastic,
light as an ice-cream scoop
with all the air inside to help it fly -

That glary-frowned at me
for grounding it so badly, from somewhere
underneath its rocky-overhanging eyebrows
  and the sockets for its eyes
  that I would poke my fingers in
  and roll big marbles in
  (when I presumed it was asleep).

I liked to hold its brain-box -
smooth and round and stitched together
like a baseball - in my palm

and tried to prise its beak apart
(to see if it would work again)
but it remained tight-lipped
and noble (nobler, true, than I)
in all its dusty flightlessness -
Still suffering my
small, delighted crimes.

I had the trap-jaw of a shark

I kept a plastic soldier in for fun -
though it was never sprung;

A fearsome crown of teeth,
new layers of them always
                waiting in the wings -
a queue, to have a go at you -
like unused razor blades
and always pointing backwards
like the seaside waves
                that tiny children scribble -
always just about to dribble.

And I realised, one day,
while staring at its jagged grin -
The only sure way out . . . .
Was still yet further in!

I had a swordfish sword

that could not be ignored - it duelled
with a peacock's feather, criss-crossed
with it, *swish-splosh,* like a coat of arms
with no-one coming to much harm -

It had its charms;
not shiny and not sharp, particularly,
it made me think
of gallant deeds beneath the sea -
my own swordfish behaving quite heroically.

Still sticky at the end
where it had been glued on;

Wondering at it, as I did, one day
I pinched my own nose
without thinking
just to make quite sure
I hadn't dropped *that*
on the floor!

I had an ammonite

that curled away into the past
as if it had no appetite for nowadays -
twisting out from underneath my gaze
but at the same time beckoning (well,
by my reckoning) with all the
crook of its eternal finger

'Come and see my limestone mud at work,
still wrapping things up nicely for geologists
to come upon six epochs later -
hidden in a *rock-potater!*'

I had some Roman Coins found scattered
in a monastery garden, along with fragments
of clay pipes that were disposable 300 years ago
in which tobacco would have burned,
some other fossils, indeterminate as far as
leaves or molluscs were concerned.

Donated to me, every one,
By Uncle Ron - who only spoke to me
that once, to pass them on.

And all displayed upon a low
and pink formica-surfaced table
that would, one day soon, upturned,
become a rapid-river raft
with legs for masts
to hold in every corner.

And if you believe *that's* daft -
then listen up. I swopped the *whole* collection ;
My museum, the Display of Wonders
that my school friends would come round to
see and tell *their* friends to come to see -
and who themselves would not forget

Just six months later

for a Lego set!

House Martians

*(our own summer aliens
making themselves at home)*

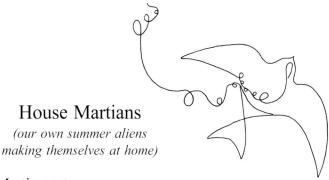

House Martin nests
Like sleeveless vests –
With only one armhole left
To struggle in-and-out-of
late for school again - these

Bee-bobbly, mud-nugget
Upside-down hives
Suddenly stuck to the Music Room wall
Like 'fridge magnets
(under the gutter) a whole row
of souvenir clutter - from
Wherever it is they have been. Now

All in a fairground knock-me-down row,
Not coconut shy
of a line of unmusical children
All queueing-up to give-it-a-go -
Not six feet below - and

Pegged-out with Martins-at-home
At the lips of their begging bowl huts
(their building-site hard hats
for pink bags of blue-
-stomach chicks)

All turning to look again
Over their shoulder at

Pink faces up-at-them
out of their grey-and-green uniforms
Just like a long string of harbour buoys
Bobbing at sea.

'Majesty's Navy birds, these are m'lads' -
Sailing school skies and
Plugging their bouncy-boat hull-holes
Like corks for the rum, for
A leaking of mutinous youngsters
too soon, over the side -
Swept away with the tide

To a sea-shanty tune
from the school Music Room.

Ginko Biloba

Too plain
for proper veins.

Simple as dinosaur brains -

it has to try to stretch both ways at
Once for all the sunlight it can see
or split itself in two

endeavouring to - does not know
how to go its Autumn colours yet,
Grows old with palest gold - the

faintest sunlight stain . . .
for all its stretchmark pains.

Press one in the pages of a book
on prehistoric life and make yourself
a crinkle-cut, crepe paper sunrise
with an hour missing, slot one leaf
inside another one the way you fit a tail
into a glider made of balsa wood

Or use it as a fan
to soothe a Brontosaurus -
or a T.Rex (if you can!)

poppyheadspoppyheadspoppyheadspoppyheadspoppyheadspoppyheadspoppy

Poppyheads

Poppyheads - bedstead knobs, that

Clack together like arthritic knuckles,
nobbly kneecaps, clumsy elbows knocking
over teacups -

Bouncing off each other
just like cardboard conkers
on the end of springy *sticks-for-strings*

and *missing* half the time!

Pale old skulls

with blue-veined temples,
light as parchment,
showing all their ribs and nodding
to be safe at home - no more

than a pinch *of hard-little-ant-egg* thoughts
Still left to them, lost, with smiles,
to any shaking of the wind - the

barely-moving air -
that draws a children's *zig-zag-circle*
on the end of every brittle, tongue-dry, twiggy
Charcoal stick.

poppyheadspoppyheadspoppyheadspoppyheadspoppyheadspoppyheadspoppy

Papier-maché pumpkin lanterns

that make you want to tap your fingernail
upon them for their *empty-sugar-packet* sound -

All jostling for a place to see
like wobbly spinning plates
kept going, one by one -
and frightened, by the colour-drained
and bony ghost of every other
lantern, like a head upon a neck

upon a pole at Traitor's Gate.

Here they wait,
unclattering,
this August afternoon
as I walk by -

Rusting downwards
from their seized-up
spinner-spanner
Corrugated roofs,

Ventilating (shutters up
and tiny archway windows wide)

For nothing but the sun
        that's dried them all

To pattern the cottage wall.

Circles
of
Gulls

Gulls are whirlpooling
    over the sky,
        casting their circles
            again and again,
                imperceptibly drifting
                    without ever seeming

to leave where they were to begin with,
    spreading themselves
        like crumbs in the butter on toast
            into corners - lassoing

whatever it is they are doing - blueing
    the white of their communal eye,
        having a slow-motion try
            at horseshoeing everyone's sun
                just for fun - suddenly

they have gone by,
    used up the whole of the sky

        without even seeming to try.

HORSECHESTNUTHORSECHESTNUTHORSE

A *Conker*
Is furniture
All of its own,

A Horse Chestnut
Button
Unsewn,

A walnut
-grain
Antique

Popped
Out of the prickly gob
-stopper cheek

Of a silk
-padded bed

To clonker 'pon
My cycle helmet

Head!

ConkersConkersConkersConkersConkers

A
(not so traditional, seasonal)

*CONKER TIME
PLAYGROUND RHYME
(with instructions!)*

*CONKERER
(person doing the conkering)
'I can clonker conker
If you keep it still -*

*ALL
Keep it dangling on your string
Until . . . until . . . until . . .'*

*(increase number of 'untils' with
each person's turn. Only when
last 'until' has been chanted may
the **Conkerer** swing his conker)*

*ALL
'He's hit it!
Has he split it?*

*No!
It's Kevin's go.'*

(obviously insert appropriate name here.
The **conkeree** *- person being conkered -*
won't always be called Kevin)

OR

'He's missed it!
Never mind.
Better luck another time.'
(No complaining if it's 'strings'. That's
just one of those conk'ry things.)

OR

'Yes! You win!
You've conkered him!
Now put the pieces in the bin.'

(The **conquering** *conkerer is now entitled*
to tie a knot in his string to signify his victory
and to declare his conker a 36er or a 99er
or, more realistically, a 2er - whatever it might
be. One or two people may need a little help
with their Maths and their sense of propriety
at this late point)

ConkersConkersConkersConkersConkers

wOoDcOckwOoDcOckwOoDcOckwOoDcOckwOoD

Woodcock

Try as you might
(that's even supposing
you might think of looking)
You simply won't see me -
For I am the colour and texture of trees
and their year after year
of fallen-down leaves -

*Though **I** can see **you***
and every last thing you do;
All of your stumbling about in the blind,
Your clodhopping crimes
in these old woods of mine, with my

Snooker-ball eyes
Rolling every-which-way
in my side-pocket sockets
for potting the trottings of foxes
        to opposite corners behind me
whilst noting the gloat of a stoat
at my camouflaged throat -

A worldful of troubles
In two tiny bubbles of
hazelnut shine. Three
hundred and sixty
degrees - and all mine.

(Focus on both of your ears
while you study the tip of your nose
and that gives you some
indication of just how my
Seeing-in-circles goes)

My ancestry is the saltmarsh sea
and the silky, lugworm, soft-shore mud -

But I've swopped my tides for these woodland rides
and the crumbling earth
                        (with your heavy-booted thud)

And the empty skies trailing seabird cries
for the jays and the jackdaws
                    and the rooks and the 'pies.

Now my waves are the breeze
                  in the oak and the beech

And I sit where no waters reach.

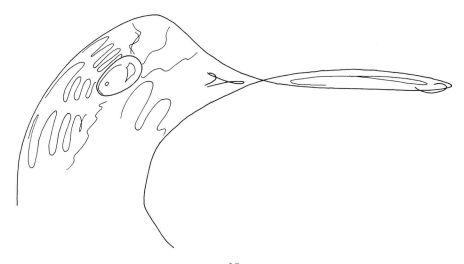

I am leaf-mould rusted,
Mushroom gilled, I
Plumb the depths
and the worm is spilled.

Count to a hundred
With your eyes wide open
and you still won't find me
'Til at least one owl has spoken,

Then I'll shake off my litter
and clamber to the skies
And you might see my silhouetted
Outline trundle by -

An easier *I Spy*
Where *every* bird's heart lies.

wOoDcOckwOoDcOckwOoDcOckwOoDcOckwOoD

Vasa

Vast, unsunken wreck
still rising, dripping
like a weary whale

to fill our eyes and her
dry dock museum, big as
any aircraft hangar;

Monstrously unburied
from her harbour silt - all her timbers
and her sailor-bones fermented

In the dark to liquorice and treacle,
pinched into resemblances
of figureheads and carvings,
spit-and-polished by four centuries
of mud and rolling skulls
between the decks -
its cannonholes like
toothless gums.

Once - all that long time ago
a shiny Swedish king
demanded something *grand*; too big
and too unplanned, she wobbled
              on her sea-legs for a moment,
Stumbled to her knees -
and even full of all her not-so-shiny people
       crowded deck to deck to floor to ceiling,
just to stop her leaning, keep her steady -

She was never ready,
fainted and keeled over
like a dinosaur - and sank,
still blowing bubbles
for another hour or two,

While all of Stockholm city
and the king and half the navy
stood by watching quietly and
looking round expectantly
for some idea of what to do.

Cradled now in tanks of open air,
kept humid so that all her planks
                        and skeletons
don't splinter deafeningly, twang apart
Along their rib-cage length,
She balances upon her keel,
her single heel, not likely
                        to tip over
for her lack of ballast anymore.

She has the floor.

And with her
worn-out water
still she drips
behind the eyes.

Sparrows Have Eroded

Sparrows have eroded
the whole white-uncut-loaf
gone-breezeblock-stale
that I left out for them

Into a miniature geology
of arches, and stacks (where
the arches have fallen) and caves
made of chalk - a

Seven Sisters Sunblest
pitted with beakmarks
where all the tiny flints
have been removed. A

Crusty weathered-wheatflour

Sussex cliff.

Mouse Bird

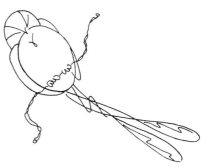

Pom-pom headed
Humbug bird
with a sunflower seed
for a beak.

Mouse birds
flushing delicately pink
with mouse-ear tink-
-ling faintnesses (like
china-chinkling waitresses)
with being slightly rushed today -

Giving the tail-tag game away -
through housy-mousy
browny-grey.

Outstretched
Crescent moons
of finger-feathers
fanning daylight
with the thinnest
-ever sound
of sticks along
the railings - flying

Like it's choppy sailing.

Swinging their tails
through the springy-
twig trees, like gymnasts
with those straight-out knees
On pommel-horse and
parallel bars - tiny
Asymmetric stars

Proving that a
Tail is best
for upside-down
Agility tests

But wearing them all the way
Over their heads . . .

When sitting on the
Humbugs in their
Roly-poly nest!

longtailedtitslongtailedtitslongtailedtitslongtailedtitslong

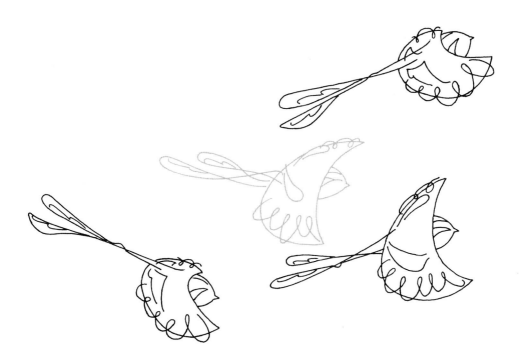

Nest of a Long-Tailed Tit
(For Turner and his Prize)

What is
This airy ball
of nothing and yet
everything - this

Rolly artwork
of ephemera?

Appliqué
of feathers and moss,
lichen and thistledown
stitched with spiders' web,
threaded with light
and hardly a sound - a

Shuttlecock collage of
flimsiest foliage fabric, a

Textile treat of half-
anticipated flight,

Smoke-drift
of seed-sift -

Its form evaporated
in a blur of barely-
focused sight.

Turner was right.

(All ye who covet
Turner's Prize
Be humbled - or
Avert your eyes!)

Curlew Haiku

Lost Curlew trio
Looking down the flagstick hole
On the golf course green.

Three beaks poking in,
Curved as openers for cans
Without their tin lid.

Curious to know
The size of any lugworm
Still at home down there!

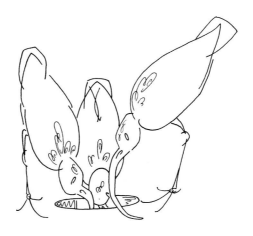

The Secret World
of
Master Geoffrey's Trees

And as I look, I see

that Geoffrey's carvings
are the Spirit of a Tree
That's looking out at me.

For years ... without me knowing,
he has sat within his root and tree-stump
Studio, coaxing out the wood's own
artistry and innuendo, all its whimsical
grotesque and ribald understanding

of itself. Upon the shelf

A gargoyle leers at me - a
giant polished conker of a
woody carbunkle as big as
any uncle's head, and gone
completely wild - and next

to that, from holes where branches
used to be (like very dislocated
shoulders) all around a bit of trunk,
A tree begins to open wide its mouth
to sing, while, curled around itself

A hibernating dragon waits for Spring,

An alder snake coils slowly down
a hazel stick to make a curly-wurly grip,

A seal basks on a rock, a mermaid
slips into the sea, gnarled fingers

play a hollow instrument
entirely new to me. And in *his* hands

the mere suggestion of a dancing sprite
becomes a dancing sprite. Watch closely;

Once he is quite sure
of each new tongue-in-cheek
Caricature, he lifts it with his chisel,
eases it into the daylight
from its
convoluted,
Arboreal world -

Midwife
at an impish birth
a hundred years from its own
struggle from the earth.

Whoever is the artist here,
Each tree is Geoffrey's gallery -
and, everywhere he can

He hides himself
a leafy-featured,
knobby-nosed
and nonchalantly
mischievously-posed
without-his-clothes . . .

Green Man!

Moorhen Stretches

Moorhen s   t   r   e   t c h e s

for the far side of the lane,
Going for it like a train,
like a ski-slope jumper landing -
Not quite understanding

all the principles at work here -

(both eyes popping out with fear
that its silly head won't manage
to traverse the road undamaged)

Unconcerned about its body
(very plump and somewhat purple
And providing all the hurtle)
F   o   l   l o w i n g   along   behind

with yellow legs like pole-vault poles
which also play a minor role

in getting it
       a c   r   o   s   s
                  in time!

The Big Snow

This snow is crowding us out -

Mugging us in our own house,
gathering us into a snowball

  of people
      and furniture,
           timbers and bricks
                  with

Big hands of wind -

Rolling us all round the garden - clinging

To places you wouldn't expect
      like the whole of one side of a wheelie bin,

raggings of spiders' web up
in the eaves of the shed
where it looks just like old bits
of Santa Claus beard,

Slipping its way down the window
like splodges of porridge
Twanged from a catapult-
Spoon. Imagining

People as snowmen,

Rooftiles as
Butterfly scales.

Heights

Born
from a height
the baby Giraffe
dropped out
like a light

taking his very first breath
on its way from the 21st floor -
hoping for straw
but finding
a
concrete
replacement
(down in the basement)

to wind him,

to knock his breath
straight out again -
his floppy new
stomach
hit
by
a runaway train -

Overdue
parcel
of long scarf and leggings
(bones gone a-begging)
all undone suddenly,
loose as dropped cutlery,
tumble of
Pick-a-sticks
never the same.

Left on his ownsome
to work out his puzzle
(with only a nuzzle)

find his own feet
in the midst
of the
muddle
and stand up
and look just the same
as his mum

way

up

there

(such a
mosaic mare)

While *we* balance
on *two*
as we gawp
and we gasp

and we stare.

How Now, The Highland Cow?

The Highland calf
is a beast and a half -

How now, the Highland Cow?

At a pinch (and
with assistance)
One will *just* fit in the bath -

(Not now, dear Highland Cow!)

You could dry your towels
Across his horns,

With the warmth of the breath
Of his Highland yawns

Though his deadpan disposition
Might be even more forlorn!

How now, the Highland Cow?

It would take you a year
To comb his coat -

How now, the Highland Cow?

So you wouldn't have the time
For a wee mountain goat -

How now, the Highland Cow?

But please resist the urge
To trim the hair from his eyes,

Though he's undercover, certainly,
He isn't in disguise -

It's an energy-free remedy
For keeping out the flies!

How now, the Highland Cow?

Pantomime
with
Turnstones

Stage-scenery clouds,
too purple to be grey,
wobble in entirety
and dangerously -
up against the light.

I have got as far
as sitting on my bottom
on the bean-bag stones
because these birds have

Let me creep and crunch
my way, quite happily,
along the shingle bank -
and now I use my heels
to drag me closer, knees both
rising and ridiculously falling -

While the turnstones
simply stand around
despite the comedy -
about as keen as all
these pebbles to move
on - still balancing the
glassy-quartzy, cobble-
colours of themselves
upon on their backs

and rusting up with
orange-iron dribbles
with the wintertime.

Sea lifts up behind them
like a running wall of storm

and falls like knuckles of a
fist behind the roaring drop.
The turnstones only fidget
in between the tons of ocean
and my trainer soles - barely

rained upon and interested
only in the feeling of the
stones-between-their-toes.

The sea slops at them
just like broken milk, they
hang about for it to go -
like empties on the step.

Camel On Rails

I came across the camel on a railway track;

A lofty wanderer with carpets on, a stately
Desert galleon with half-lid eyes on some horizon
I half-turned to see -
Out of its sandy depth on rails.

Children swarmed the iron and the sleepers,
Pulling their donkeys up the banks to see, and
                                        all the while the
Camel man was pleased to hold him for me -
So I focused their expressions
As the train came down the line.

Then, as the pompous policeman (out for the
day to make sure we stayed upon our bicycles)
                            began to wave and shout for us to
Come on down the slope -
And children scattered at his voice and uniform
(Not at the fast-approaching train!)
The camel slowly turned to see, still
Chewing on his bridle, while my nut-faced
Nomad kept his smile upon me 'til I'd finished
                                        and then
  Nodded an unhurried grace upon our meeting. Bedouin

And camel wandered over - sandalled
Feet and giant plodding pads
Between the lines - now hidden

As the goods train separated us
By five whole minutes - gone and almost

Lost to view beyond the
Settled noise and dust - the

Two of them belonging

To another time, at
One another's pace.

Egret

Waits among hooves for an hour
To pick a solitary tick
From a donkey's lashes.

Jumps - a nodding plume of white
Upon a helmet-shine of water.
Standing in the reeds to soft attention, rises,

Indolent, to blur the blue above the Nile;
A pharaoh's feather-ghost umbrella
Cradling the Sun.

Fills a tree with candles
Which will dab a chalk-slick of reflection
On the drifting gloom.

antzanaphidzantzanaphidzantzanaphidzantzanaphidzantz

How Now, Green Aphid?

A half a million ants
are counting themselves
up and down the silver birch
both ways at once
like chocolate vermicelli
with antennae

Going to and from their milking
- silky beads of honeydew
from herds of aphid cows
(with not-a-moo between 'em
and every one a green'un)

Out to pasture
on their flimsy
landing-pads-for-hoverflies
that if you flip -
are silver birch leaf fields
for grazing upside-down;

Funny milk
from *ant*i-gravi*tickled*
clowns.

antzanaphidzantzanaphidzantzanaphidzantzanaphidzantz

BarbaryApeBarbaryApeBarbaryApeBarbaryApeBarbaryApe

Lookout

'You're on my island.
Do not Disturb!

Well, yes, disturb me
with a banana, if you like
But don't expect me
to smile at the camera -
I'm busy. I'm guarding
The Straits of Gibraltar -
Directing the Shipping
(as well as unzipping
bananas) keeping an eye
On the bit of a gap that
Allows people, cap-in-hand,
into **The Mediterranean**
(No-one *too* a l i e n
you understand). 'Cos we
Can't turn it off like a tap.
That there's the north coast of
Africa. Over here's Spain.
Now, let me explain -
See **The Atlantic?** Well,
Call me pedantic, but I'm
watching each one of its
incoming waves - for
height and for depth -
to make sure it behaves.
If I'm getting annoyed
It's because I'm employed
(as we have been for
hundreds of years -
with our barbary beards)

To watch from **The Rock**
for invasion or shock.
(Dolphins don't count -
they're *always* about) and
If you distract me *the*
Worse it might well be -

For if We never falter . . .
Gibraltar won't alter.'

Now He's A
Customs & Excise
Officer!

The Barbary Ape
Stops us at the checkpoint.

'Your bag is difficult -
Open it for me, please.
As I thought - exploding
Banana - this will have to be
confiscated, I'm afraid.

Sorry - don't do cute. No,
not interested in a conversation
Or holding your little finger
for you. Pose for the camera? Hmm.
You'll have to be quick - I'm working.
This is my best side. Nothing
else that's halfway edible?

Taps me sharply
On the side of the nose
Without even looking.

'O.k. You can go. I've finished
*with you for the moment. **Move***
***Along.** Next please. It's*

Rude to stare. Ban-
-ana to declare?'

OystercatchersOystercatchersOystercatchers

Beaky Billingtons

The Beaky Billingtons
Are giving us a black (and white)
Eye in the ear. Nosey-

Shoreline-parkers
Busybodying each plover, gull and avocet
Into its birdy sort-and-set -
Shuffling flocks
To keep apart the dry and wet.

Making a beeline
To sharpen the stripes of the sea
Separating water -
Tidily.

Kicking up a fuss
(undoubtedly because of us)
At every shell and pebble
We have the temerity to walk upon
As if they were somebody's egg,

Vetting every piece of driftwood
(rope or bottle, bit of weed)
For any dregs of usefulness
And leaving it a slightly different mess.

Look at this one!
Clattering its cheap, red plastic beak
Like non-stop chopsticks
Or those sweetie-scoops for Pic&Mix
To always overfill a paper bag

And another!
Marching militarily along the shingle bank,
Assuming its importance
With a badly-tempered swank.

Grumpy old men
On a black and white telly, all
Untanned seaside legs and rolled-up trousers,
With their hanging-from-a-thread, their
Loosely-buttoned rage-red
Victor Meldrew eye -

Filling up the empty sky
with 'Getaway! Oi! Getaway!'
For lack of anything more sociable to say.

This one's gone pneumatic!
Hammering off a limpet -
(stuck with all its eyes-tight might
and minding its own business)
Flying off in triumph with it
like a little sticky-footed Chinese hat
Clamped upside-down in two-tone
Tongs as if it were a coal -

Still managing to broadcast
Far and wide
To every living soul. And
Here's the last one of the day -

The obligatory Beaky B
Waiting not-so-patiently
Up on the clifftop's 18th tee

For two last golfers in the evening light,
Making sure (by keeping score)
There's no-one left up on the golf-course
Overnight.

* 'Beaky Billington' is an old Derbyshire expression for somebody who can't seem to help poking their nose into other people's business!

Float

Be a Fulmar Petrel. Float.

Go on. Be a

Mini-albatross -

One wing snipping plantains
all along the clifftop edge,

The other scoring a horizon,
Separating Sea from

Sky. So

Go on. Try. Be a

Fulmar Petrel.

Float - to Fly.

PIERpierPIERpierPIERpierPIERpierPIERpierPIER

PIER

A good idea is a pier -
Longer by far than it might first
appear . . . on a
Postcard view
*'Wishing **here were you**
on Holiday too' -*
(which you would be
if you were me).

A good idea is a pier
For allowing your own legs
To not disappear
Up to more than their knees
(then your ears, by degrees!)
When you want to keep walking
This far out to Sea -
Just to see.

A good idea is a pier
If you want to imagine
(providing it's clear)
The coastline of France -
Though from here there's no chance!
Lean as far as you like
From the lifeboat house -
(Lifeboat inside like a mouse)
And you still won't see much
*that's not Belgian, Norwegian
- or Dutch!*

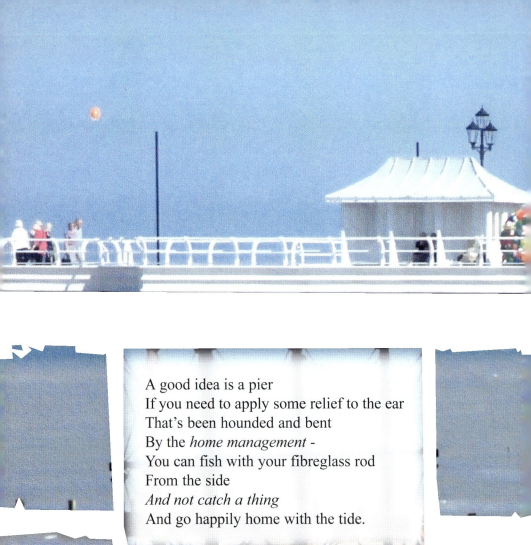

A good idea is a pier
If you need to apply some relief to the ear
That's been hounded and bent
By the *home management* -
You can fish with your fibreglass rod
From the side
And not catch a thing
And go happily home with the tide.

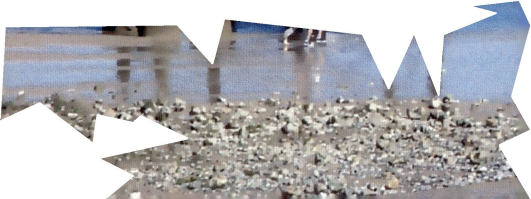

A good idea is a pier
If you quite like to frighten yourself
(with some fear)
By staring in awe
At the swirl and the maw
of the boiling green sea
Round the old iron legs *be-*
-tween two of your own -
And the floorboards
An inch or two further apart
Than at home!

A good idea is a pier
If you fancy some candy floss (or a beer)
or you'd quite like to ask the man with balloons
If he'll notice you soon
So that you can let go of one
All on your own
And watch 'til it disappears . . .
(sailing the sky for years)

Still being blown.

A good idea is a pier
If you like your hair sideways
(and not quite so near)
With a gale whistling
Straight up the North Norfolk coast -
Head back and arms open wide,
Making the most
Of no shelter at all
In the nose-bending
Teeth of the squall.

This last verse
Might well not be here.
It's only because
I hold *Sheringham* dear
I'm reluctant to make it
So perfectly clear
That where *Cromer's* concerned
This poem's well-earned . . .

A good idea
Is a pier!

A Guillemot On Sheringham Beach

Alien as a penguin
springboarded
from a melting iceberg -

Sat, all on his own,
just like a lonely circus act
with suit-sleeve flippers
                    for his wings
held at the crease
       in readiness to flap,
uncertain
as a cricket bat - unkindly

Heckled to perform by jeers of gulls,
Ringed by groynes and pebbles
and binoculars with faces to them,
Sand for sawdust, waves
for tent flaps opening and
closing, promenade steps
for tiers of filling seats.

But guillemot has no circus trick

Except to wonder where he is
And why it was . . .
. . . that stormy wind and rain conspired to
Pluck him from the middle of the sea
(and half-a-million bobbing corks of other guillemots)
and only he - to whirl him to the sky and drop him,

Toss him, wave to spray-torn wave,
against his beating paddle-wings
and dump him at the storm's end in the
early morning dark on someone else's beach.

'His feet are stuck!' cries someone
as the swilling sand makes moats
and sucks his webby toes
into a pair of sloppy pools.

*'Is he exhausted? Is he old?
Don't the others like him anymore?'* Then

All at once he seems to hear the Sea.
Stares for seconds over first one shoulder
                            then the other,
Pulls a foot free, absent-mindedly,
Unhindered by the laugh of little boys
at its sink-plunger sucking noise,
Twists around and waddles seaward,
Dragging out the other after him, and
Slapping both big feet a six-inch
                    ruler's length ahead of him
Like frogmen's flippers
Smacking at the silky sand -

He marches out into the sea.

Wades (like we do
when the water gets too deep) by
Swinging chicken-thighs from side to side
through wavelets and more ribby wavelings

'Til the water rises
and then falls without
so much as breaking

And he settles on it
Like a little bathtub toy -
all tidily - and bobs

Back out to Sea

Where all the other
Guillemots must be.

Owlzanbatz

A bat I spotted
looped and knotted
my October sky

still light enough
to see the evening
through its sails -

Ringed nicely-prizely
by a set of
One-inside-the-other
Fairground hoops

of early 'Don't
Disturb Me'
Tawny Owly

H O O T S

Discerning the Fern

You can learn to discern a fern
(though the sound of it it lackens
the smacken of 'bracken')

I am foolishly fond of this frond;
(whether sunk in a bouldery dip like a pond
or riding a dark-green hillsidy sea)
Its flip-floppy sharks' teeth
Do not bother me. *Inevitably*

Curled centipedes of vertebrae
on bendy-over backbones, all
Strumming on my knee, hedge-

Clipping all the sheep-snip paths
with *zig-zag* stitching, up the fells,

Sweeping up behind me their own
needles; each a herring-bony
mini-Christmas tree - though
hardly *ever*green - they're

Browning here already on my desk,
Rustling-up a music with the rusty
Iron tines of certain instruments
such as *karimbas* that you
Pluck with fingernails. They are the
Curling fingers of a baby looking
for a grown-up one to grasp -

The one that's at this very task!

Saxophone Player

Who is this untucked-
-shirted little man-in-bud
Playing the plastic saxophone;
Fingering the bright red keys
To try to make a difference
to the helpfully (though not so
very musically) incorporated
Party-hooter buzz.

He has the Jazz Club cap, that subtle
Swaying of the knees (both
aiding and abetting) while already he is
Staring out beyond the frightening
Blare to happier possibilities
With sound. Alas -

His plastic saxophone
Lays in its case (a toybox
full of cars and jigsaw bits) un-
-hindered now for years. This

Little music man
Became a fully-stretched-and-sweat-wet
T-shirt drummer, knocking every kind of
Rhythm off the walls and ceiling
of a crowded cellar, loosening
the very ribs inside your chest, pinning back
Your ears to fill your heart and soul
With newly-quarried rock and roll. His

Fingers twirling split-end drumsticks these days -
And a Bass drum pedal for those keys -
But no mistaking that same
Manic-minstrel

Music in the knees!

Don't Let Your Grandma Get Away!

Don't let your Grandma (or your Grandpa
for that matter)
Get away -

Without them telling you
At least *one* story from
		when *they* were little -
Everyday!

My own mum
is a grandma
of considerable expertise

And yet
she's only just remembered (if you please)
that my *Great* Grandma
(that would be *her* Grandma too)

		Lived in a house
		that had a *tunnel* from the cellar
		underground, that led eventually
		Into a *Castle* by the sea -
		So bands *of smugglers* could land
		and roll their barrels full *of contraband*
		Through *caves* (that doubled-up
		as an escape route to the beach
		for poor, besieged nobility) -
		Sneak through the *dungeons,*
		Up Great Grandma's tunnel
		And be home in time for *tea!*

Good Heavens!
I'd expect to hear a tale
like that one
by the time
that I was *7!*

(Not 51 -
when most
of the excitement's
been and gone)

Dental Scandal

£5.84
For 9 old teeth!

When you pay
just the same price
for a Checkup
if you've got *a full set*
of them still -

That's nearly 65p
for each tooth!
When someone
in their prime

is only paying
14p a time
for all their 42!

I think it's
scandalous -
I do.

Without My Auntie Ruth

Without my Auntie Ruth
There'd be no photographs
of me when I was young - no
Snapshots *of a me I* hardly recognise
(with half a century's disguise)
in shorts and mostly miserable
with being asked to stand,
or sit upon a baby brother's rug
when I had *other* plans - ***in***

1957 black-and-white (when
you could not record the colours
that you were and everyone
was happier with shades of grey -
or so they tell me, anyway).

She didn't make a thing of it
but partway through a summer's
                            afternoon
(approaching tea-time, not *too* soon)
Her Brownie camera appeared;

a one-eyed black enamel caddy
(that's a tea tin) and the leather
satchel (that's a schoolbag) box
you kept it in - with its own little window
that you looked down into so that
you could see somebody straight ahead
(a retro-periscope, it might be said)
- when all they saw of *you* though
was the crowning of your head!

Then back we went
(by sisterly consent)
against the brick wall, usually
with promises of something
nice for tea (no firing squad,
you see) or posed with
birthday presents, **happily!**

So here I am, then
having some small hand
in Auntie Ruth's
recording of the fact

that when I was this old
I had a three-wheeled scooter
on which I would doubtless play

*And **this** is what I looked like -*

On that memorable day.

Tonsils

I had my tonsils out -

I wasn't told about it
'Cos my mum knew very well
That I would shout about it
All the way to hospital

and back - and so we packed
A suitcase. 'What's this for?' I said.
'Oh, just in case -' my Mum replied.
A small brown one, it was.
I stared at it because
it didn't seem quite big enough
for all Mum's things *and* mine - for
Both of us to have a lovely time.

(I knew I hadn't gone to school as usual
of course, but didn't want to draw
attention to the fact unnecessarily -
as it was *not* where I'd prefer to be)

And off we went.

'Mum, have I had an accident?'
I queried as we pushed
the ward doors open wide.

'No, not exactly, Dear.
You're here to have your tonsils out -' my
Mum replied and once inside
Confided in me further.
'And you're staying overnight as well.
I didn't dare to tell you on the bus
because I knew you'd make enough fuss
For the two of us.'

There was a moment's silence
while the news sank in.
'But I don't want a little operation!
*Mum - I promise **I'll be good***
From now on!' I began to howl.

The consternation and the din
Brought Sister and another nurse
In at the double and it
took the three of them
(was I *really* worth the trouble?)
Just to get my striped *pyjamas on*
While I made far more noise
Than if the hospital *alarm was on!* I

Yelled myself to sleep.
My tonsils were removed
without a peep.

However much
I might, up to that point,
have been to blame,
It is what happened next
that is the cause of
My *eternal* shame. The

Morning afterwards, and
Knowing that my throat
was bound to feel a little sore, a
Kind nurse crept in quietly, and
Left a Mivvi (Strawberry,
it was) for me - and me alone -
and softly closed the door.

I let that ice cream
Melt inside its wrapper
'Til it swam around its lollystick
Because I still felt cross.

The nurse came in again.
I looked up at her
Sad and puzzled face.

And to this very day
I'm sorry for my selfish trick,
for my disgrace - and
Absolutely no-one

Else's loss.

Xmas Tonsils

Wobbly wishbone-like
and bladder-rubbery as
Self-inflated mistletoe.
Not anywhere
That I would like to go
To have a Christmas kiss!
'No thank you,
Auntie Glad. I
Think I'll give this
One a miss!'

Les The Barber

Les the Barber
knows a thing or two - it's true;
his Barber's Shop
is choc-a-bloc with history -
and full of barbery antiquities . . .

   . . . like cut-throat razors (that
would hardly graze you) shaving
brushes (little walruses) and blades
still in their tiny-posty packets, powder-
puffing bulbs (like old car horns) and *my
own* favourites - hand-held trimmers
that look heavyweight enough to leave
a garden path from nose to nape - though
all they did was tidy up your neck - and
tickle you like heck! Advertisements
for everything to do with Gents;
short back and sides with **Brylcreem** shine
to make a bloke look smart - and
get his comb out, full of good intent.

Les, the Barber
knows a thing or two - it's true;
he goes to watch The Hammers
when the clamour at the door for haircuts
has died down (though Upton Park's their
ground and that's in London town!) . . .

. . . his fund of football stories in the news
will keep you properly amused
*(he'll not get so excited that your hair
becomes ignited!)* He'll ask you
all about your team and matches
that you might have seen (on telly, though
you might have *been)* managers
and recent signings - multi-million dollar
football players whining about pay (on this
he'll have *a lot* to say!) He'll listen *to your*
point of view with interest, unless . . .
it's Arsenal or Spurs that you profess
to follow - in which case, *'down you get -
we'll try again tomorrow!'*

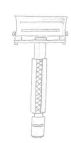

Les the Barber
knows a thing or two - it's true . . .
. . . and while you're sitting in his chair
(no need at all to say your prayers!)
you'll soon begin to see why *hair* -
or cutting it, to be precise,
is what he specialises in -
and pretty soon a huge reflected grin
will spread from ear to ear
(remember them?) and all your fears
evaporate . . . so . . .

Whether it is *balding pate* -
'nice trim and polish, mate?'
or *hardly old enough to make a date
with Father Christmas* - barely
poking from the sheet and
looking very sweet,
(head turning round to Mum
just like a cherry on a bun) . . .

Once underneath the siren spell
of snipping scissors
(and the comb)
He's time *for you*
and you alone.
(he'll not take orders
on the phone!)

You'll walk tall with the best of 'em
From Les' Hair Emporium,
Proud that Les had asked you
What you best *like to be called* -
(which may not be the same
as what they gave you as a name)
And never, ever -
(Almost never)

*Hardly **ever** bald!*

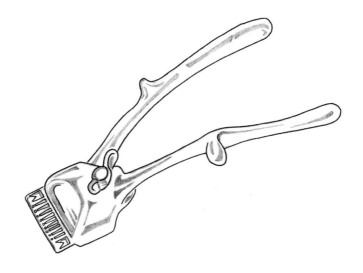

The Squirrel Man

The Squirrel Man

Comes true each morning
Early, his back door -
the first blink of an eye.

Wet grass soaks his feet.
He stops to touch
a single drop of rain
that hangs upon the crimped
and crooked cage wire -

Notes it quickly fill
and ripen, watery
with rusty reds and oranges
long before the Sun
Is fizzing in the mist;

A squirrel is bounding
all around the inside of
its safe enclosure, corner to
Corner, to corner him, bouncing

like the little red dot
Over music notes
you might follow on tv -

A furry flare of ear and tail
that holds him always
In its detail.

He knows which one it is,
just like he knew his Children
when he taught them all that time.

Each day his heart is won again, all over -
Found here, held here, opened, like the
Hazelnut the squirrel holds and
Turns and turns to find the

grain of. Squirrel Man,
inside his tie and tweedy jacket,
Squeezes sideways in with it
and makes it welcome -

Ducking snappy twigs and head-bump branches that
The squirrel barely touches . . .

. . . to be gone again and whispering the wire
with tiny toes and fingers -
like a ripple over Hempton Pond.

'Be an expert -'
Someone told him, as a boy.
*'Find One Thing to believe in
and know everything there is to
Know about it, then your life will be
Extraordinary - and each moment Singular.'*

One day, a schoolmate
Brought a dead Red Squirrel
Into class; a traffic
Accident, though

Squirrel Man had never seen
A thing so rarified and true
and even in its death -
It caught away his breath;

It lit a flame
Among the tiny conifers
Of chair-and-table legs and
All day long he followed it and
Blew upon it, fanning
That first vision of it and

Imagining it
Jumping up upon
His schoolboy knees -

And there he knew

he'd found
His expertise.

RedSquirrelRedSquirrelRedSquirrelRedSquirrel

At Derwentwater

A small brush fire
Suddenly sparked
From the conifer tinder,

Sprang - a
trampled-puffball
Burst of rust,
Across a path -

To stop halfway to
Juggle a cone.

Like a shuttle on a loom
She throws her quick life
From one side to the other, one
Side to the other,

Light-leaping now
As a sneezing of nutmeg to
Crackle dead wood
In the farside trees - a

Skittering sideways
Flare-in-the-wind,
Making no sense

Of a forestry
Fire-break gap.

Storm At Sea

1

Already the wind
is spoiling for a fight -
putting up its dooks
of bare-knuckle cloud.

Tougher-still tugs
Drag this whole big boat away
Out of Southampton Water, crossing
her bows to pull her round,
Crossing back over again, crossing
their fingers behind their back -

And leaving her
New and knowing no-one
in the middle of this
Empty-playground Sea.

Midging the gantries on the docks
Starlings fly pennants of small wings -
a shifty apology
of a ticker-tape
goodbye.

2

The Isle of Wight
Now slowly heaves its back for us
against the growing gale awhile,

Until the open sea begins to rise
and under cover of the dark
The eager wind
Discovers us alone
without a single star or moon.

Night crowds us suddenly - nudges
at our elbows all along the rail, stubs out
the last of our excitement and so
face to undone face, we turn to
Shoulder through the hatch.

3

Our ocean liner digs
and plunges deep
to find a stillness in the
thickening cold - enough

to steady her; nine decks
out of the fourteen
Lost to sight already.

She shudders and she kicks back hard
and suddenly her panoramic glass
Is only there to hold the lights
punched all along the sides
            from one end to the other of us.

4

At midnight, in the Crow's Nest bar
Canute, the king, is at the jazz piano
Laying down a mood
of whimsical and cool
To keep the sea

from lapping at our table-legs.
I leave him smiling grimly
at his toppling keyboard dominoes
- determined not to syncopate or
Rock and roll with it;

He reminds me too much
of the string quartet that played on
'til Titanic finally went down.

I notice
in the outside darkness
There's another ship, just like ourselves,
a mile or so away -
Jumping up *our* window - bottom
to the top
and back again - some
Storm
that must
be having!

5

I go and force the door
onto the top deck
Open - stand there.

I am in an empty ballroom
with its ceiling a collapsing sky - or
a deckchair-tumbleweeded street
in a deserted wild-west town - the
Wind careering, senseless with it,
from one corner to the next,
Wrapping itself, draughty, round my legs.

I quickly think, *'we are too big to sink -'*
until I hear the sound
of one whole ton of water smashing
Up against the side of something far too close
      and turn to find it -

Spotlit from below and slopping one end
of the swimming pool to leave the other
Empty to its sea-green tiles - returning as a
Silent tidal wave
to break upon the decking,
Spin the hapless sunbeds round
upon its overlapping deck-quoit swirls.

Flattening my clingy-T-shirt-back against the ship
I shuffle sideways, inching my eyeballs
over the side. White water

Flees the ship -
Clambering in panic
Up the heaving flanks of ocean,
Hardly getting any sort of grip
before it's sliding all the way back down again -
Shooting a glance at me over its shoulders,

Way over my own head height.

My heart is sinking. There are souls
I need to think of saving.

6

I make my way as best I can
along the gangway;
one whole quarter of a mile
of deep-pile passageway
From aft to forward, the far end
nothing more
than a miniature
Alice-in-Wonderland
Door. One moment

I am light as air
and walking on no carpet . . .
with the ship gone out from under me -

Too heavy for myself and buckling
at the knees, the next!

I lurch against my cabin door
and wonder how much seasickness
it's possible to store, crawl to my bunk
to die where I lie - too wretched
To care if we're sunk.

7

Deep in the sleep of the night
I wake at the top of the big ship's roll -
Hold-on to the sides of my bed
as she plunges -
Waits at the top again,
Plunges and waits.

Breathing like a whale, she is
Filling the hole in the Sea
    that she makes for herself with each rising,
By suddenly sliding all the way down
on her wobbly fairground rails.

At the end of her next deep lurch
She lifts and she holds too long -
So the whole Sea pounds
Both sides of her at once -
To fill in with the weight of all of it
Where she should never be.

I realise this isn't good for me.
I squeeze a hand
which squeezes back -

Our words - all lost at Sea.

8

All night long her great propellers
Wrestle with the depths

Then leap to shoot the shallows -
as they free themselves each time -

before the engines grind
to make them slowly
Turn again
and churn
the heavy
water
out be
-hind.

9

Rolling from my bed,
I creep up through the belly
of the ship-
To find grey daylight seeping,
Gather rain-soaked air
to still my stomach at the rails,

Feel marginally comforted -
At least the night survived.

Spray batters at my eyelids
Though I squeeze them open
(as and when I can)
to watch it in the wind like 'powder fuses
Zipping all along the line of waves,
Ripped up into ropes of twisty water
with each gust of gale -
And shaken into steam.

I lean a little over,
Dare a look behind.

The Sea is clinging to Us
with her Bay of Biscay netting -
Spangled white and minty green
with depths brought to the surface -
Frayed as nerve-ends
and all nylon-dishcloth stringy
with our slight escaping. The Sea

is clawing back at us, still
Clawing at us, clawing

Us back
Into the night
and the Storm . . . ***but***

All too late, for

Someone else is up on deck now, jogging,
and the light is growing so that I can see
how many bouncy-orange lifeboats there are for us. In
the restaurant windows gulls reflect themselves
and looking through them I can see that
there are breakfasts on their way. My

Trepidation tip-toes into faint excitement -

Wasn't this
Supposed to be
Our holiday?!

Sea Shrugs
(and plays for us)

Sea shrugs

increasing -
and diminishing.

Performing short percussive works;

Rolling out a foot-pedalling blur
Of big bass drum, building up a cymbal
Crash (its rim at the horizon), running white knuckles
over the washboard ridges of waves, driftwood sticks

Along promenade railings
with zoetrope terns -

Bar after rhythmical bar
All along its length and back.

Dragging the whole thing out over pebbles;

Seething maracas
and Chinese bells.

Sleepyflies

Big fat bottle-bank flies -

Metallic green and blue -

are banging up against
my open window,
thumping their own heads
again and again at it,

Blundering about
in all this unexpected warmth.

Too dozy to remember
who they are
and what it is they do.

Still trying to get in. Buzz-
-talking. Sleep

Flying (not walking).

flycraneflycraneflycraneflycraneflycraneflycraneflycranefly

Daddy-Long-Legs

Dances badly on the ceiling. So

Touchingly serious about its circus act, I
almost want to watch. Mistakenly
Billed as the 'Maestro of the High-wire', it is un-
co-ordinated as a clown. Its only rhythm,

a finger-licking persistence with the light bulb.

Cotton-thread legged; the technology of
Flour-paste and fuse-wire - not even
proper glue (the legs fall off too easily)

Not even the kindness of a silicon chip
Stuck in its head as an afterthought. Un-

Programmed for even the odd evasive action
that *might hearten a species* to try to evolve. No
Hint of an instinct. Just wall-to-wall cobwebs
and life-long bewilderment. *Such*

Little insistence at its own existence!

Microlight flying-machine
Full of design faults. Patented quite by mistake. The
Prototype of a jumbled mind - the blueprint
of some impetuous aviator absently

Translated into junk. Given-up-upon
and left to fend for itself. Already on the shelf

Preposterously
Ugly - its extruded plastic
machine-shop moulded
Face, expressionless
as the mouthparts of a car:

Like a pipefish (if you've seen one) and just as
Inoffensive. Always delicately poised
to lose its confidence and fall

Groping, down the wall.

Easy to catch. Snatch!
It flickers in your fisted hand -

Switching its life off and on
Before you boot it out
into the crowded Daddy-
Long-Legs night.

Is in again - for sure

Before you've time
to close the door!

flycraneflycraneflycraneflycraneflycraneflycraneflycranefly

Chin-Up Stoat

Chin-up Stoat
Rabbit bouncing
at his throat -
Buoy, to keep them
both afloat.

Trotting, high-step
'Cross the road,
(little clockwork
legs unbowed)
Managing his
Neck-scruff load
like an epiglottle
Toad - warm fur
Pouch where
Bones are stowed!

Mustelid, turned
Tip-toe Centaur.
No-go grass-grow,
Dainty Predator.

In the Eye of the Hare

I stood in a hare's eye - bulging
in alarm and surprise -

Soaping the huge orange globe of it
with a distorted picture of myself
(such as you might see
on a brass or silver doorknob)
- in running vest and shorts,
my head bent backwards
to meet up with my feet
In the shine

While it shrank in its fur
in the grass
by the fieldside gate
and waited for me
Not to have noticed it there
with its terrified stare
Which I had.
Which it knew.
Until neither of us could pretend
That I hadn't
One whole moment more

And it
Suddenly tore
from the scalp of the field
A whole turf of grass
with its back-pedal feet
to fling at me
- earth in my teeth -
Scudding the rest of itself
Over the rise of the pasture in
Fits and in starts

of
Such
Dodging and ducking-and-diving;
Skediddle-skedaddle
skedaddle-skediddle
To peel off

The watery-transfer of me on its eyeball

And sit on a hill in the middle
with ears erect,
Opening-closing
as gardening shears
In surprise at itself

And at me
Unaccountably,
Suddenly

Whirling around in the dark of its pupil -
Manageably
(no more the size of me)
Stamped, upside down,
On the wet of its retina
(Gnat in a teardrop)

Turned again
Slowly
in furrows of wondering,

Harebrained
and holy.

McGuffie's Toyshop

Our toyshop was McGuffie's -
a place where *'quite enough'* is
never quite enough at all
when you are not that tall;

It wasn't, all those years ago, in 1963
for Mark and Me, most certainly -
our noses up against the window,
leaving snail trails, toy to toy
like dot to dots along the outside
of our glass *Box of Delights* -
excitement rising at the door, we
looked at one another to be sure
and couldn't wait a moment more.

A little bell announced you -
Found you out at once if
you had come in just to look
or only with enough to buy
a plastic farmyard animal or
single penny box of caps.

Nobody came. The first trial safely through.
'Could breathe again. The sudden high-street
blare was shut away and you were all-at-once

Included. Stifled, with McGuffie's hush.

(the choosing of a toy was hallowed
and should not be rushed) -
Each unsold toy

Alive with so much stillness
practised through the hours of schooltime -
and the very thought of us. Airfix models

(cheaper ones hung in their packets on a pegboard
by the door) were light as sparrows' shoulder blades
inside their boxes and might catch you by the elbow -
galleons and Boeing aeroplanes, tanks in
camouflage and only slightly scaled-down
racing motorcycles.

Varnished wood and rosy-cheeked, wide-eyed
and laughing-at-you puppets, with their heads
too large and on one side and disappointingly
uninteresting bodies underneath their costumes,
(two blocks of wood and I suppose a dozen
hook-and-eye connected lengths of dowel) all
dangling loose as coppers-in-your-pocket
from their strings - hard to forget
McGuffie marionettes.

Plastic knights in plastic armour on their
little metal greenery, all battled-out already,
laying in a tumble, clutching onto shields and
swords and maces - one still bravely holding
high an eagle flag that flutters in a plastic wind -
all rummaged through and shivering with their
shocks inside their 'Britains Figures' box.

Doorstep cardboard sandwiches of Cluedo
and Monopoly, Ludo and Compendiums of Games
that promised more than they could possibly
contain, cold metal trains and
trial-and-error, link-together plastic carriages

(like empty Fairy Liquid bottles) with their
                                    rattly wheels
that wouldn't line up all the same -
Out on display on slot-in steely tracks
of different gauge (according to your age) - a
Tantalising world of perfect miniature
                        in which to lose yourself

And on the shelf in rows and rows
up higher than the tip of toes,
all neatly pigeonholed - were Dinky cars and
Corgi cars parked safely in their garage boxes,
some of them with diecast engines under
                                    fingernail-tight
lift-up boots and bonnets, polo-rubber-tyred
for real and illustrated like a cigarette card,
numbered - halfway there to being sold.

Cheery-cheap fluorescent rubber skeletons,
jokes and magic tricks and moulded-plastic
horror masks to waste our money on entirely
every single birthday - and
to put us both to shame, each year the same -

A giant Traction Engine
on the glass-top counter
that was not for sale -
beside which every other toy
or game, Meccano set or Lego,
model lorry, car or plane.

Went limp and pale.

For two whole weeks before a birthday
(and a month, at least, for Christmas)
We would plan the spending of our pennies
(providing we were good enough for any!)
with special visits to perouse McGuffie's wares
(as if we didn't know by heart
                              exactly what was there!)
The one of us whose birthday it was not
agreeing heartily with beaming smiles at each
                              suggested toy
To keep in with the Birthday Boy -

Our trips made all the more exquisite
by the annual dilemma as to whether
it should be *one* decent present, ie.
castle with a drawbridge, knights in residence,
or *several dozen* Matchbox Cars (we'd

been in for the catalogue on one of our
Newsagents first, for comics days -
both looking round to make quite sure
for half an hour or more before
we fingered one from off the counter pile
beneath McGuffie's baleful gaze.
'10p' he'd say - and Mark would pay.
It was *my* birthday, anyway!)

One June, with no-one's birthday likely soon,
We hit upon a plan to neatly bypass
saving-up *or* annual festivities
by offering to Guffie (Mr A. M c)
our varied (untried) services
for not exactly free - but in return for toys.

'Two willing boys,
with references to come.'

He took us on.

So, all one Saturday
(racing home for lunch and
beating one another back, excitedly)
We trampled cardboard boxes
in the concrete yard behind the shop
until a flat-pack mountain of them
teetered like a badly-shuffled pack of cards
or pile of comics, to the top of our beloved toyshop
prison wall. At half past five, well-exercised
and breathless with anticipation
we presented ourselves for inspection.

'You still here?' McGuffie frowned.
(He seemed to have forgotten us or
hoped we'd got fed up and gone)
The poor man sighed and turned
the *Open* sign to *Closed.* 'I s'pose
You'd better choose a toy -' he said.

Any *toy?!* (We each knew
what was in the other's head)
'One of these -' he added,
nodding at the cheapest Airfix models
overlapping in their packing on the door.

He unhooked two. 'Here - these'll do.'

We stared and mumbled
disappointedly . . . 'Thanks, Mr. G -

Does that include the glue?'

Home From School

That delicious feeling;

of the back door
Giving way
beneath your hand

When nothing else
worked for you
(friends *or* lessons)
quite so easily all day as

This cool, squeaky handle.

Someone here for you
who's worn that handle smooth
from coming in and out for you

(shopping, hanging out your washing,
getting it back in, making sure the mice
you made a cage out of an apple box for
haven't found their way out yet again - needing
to be fed and loose inside the outside shed!)

One whole school day
all behind you - and still
(count them) ***sixteen hours***
Of your very own

At home.

Late Harvest
*(Or how the **Cover** came about!)*

We didn't know if this would work;
Your fist a vase for all the stalk-ends
of our homemade sheaf of wheat -
(arranged most naturally). Both hoping
it would pass for something like a field
at harvest-time (before the stubble-scorch).

You holding it up high
like an Olympic torch.

Me letting loose a single Harvest Mouse
which zipped just like a caterpillar spark
on Guy Fawkes' powder trail
(with flick of tail) then went to ground.
To hide - all fizzled out -

From combine harvesters,
No doubt.

We waited for him to appear for photographs -
afraid that our stage scenery had fooled
our harvest mouse too well - quite reasonably,
one might suppose. (It was a fine
Autumnal stook.) And even though
you shook it like a wind about to blow,
                                    it seemed

He simply wasn't one of those
Who love to strike a pose.

But then you turned your nut-brown hand
to simulate a seasonal rotation (mostly
just to see if he was on the other side!) And
much to our elation, well, he seemed to like the ride!
Took us - whiskers, toes and fingers,
                                  ears and eyes -

Completely by surprise

As if to tell us, 'Pardon me, but actually . . .

If I'm to get a sunrise -
Well, the World spins *anti*-clockwise!'

teasingteaselsteasingteaselsteasingteaselsteasingteaselsteasing

Sue's Teasels

I looked out of my bedroom window
and there was neighbour, Sue,
Doing in the early frost
The sort of thing that I might do -

Taking photographs of teasels;

    frozen cold and prickled tight,
    like airy hedgehog eggs
    all needled white and

    bending over from a
    standing-on-a-chair-seat
    height, with all their frosty weight

    to see what she had found to see
    before they sprang back, thawed -
    to teasel her, elastically -

And it was all too late.

teasingteaselsteasingteaselsteasingteaselsteasingteaselsteasing

*

On August 10th 1628 a brand new Super-Galleon, the Vasa, capsized and sank in Stockholm harbour just a few minutes after setting out on her maiden voyage - simply because she was too big and too full of people.

On board were not only crew members but their families as well, all out to enjoy the celebrations. At least 50 people drowned in sight of the helpless quayside crowds.

When the Swedish king, Gustavus Adolphus II, heard of the disaster he was not very pleased. The Vasa was to have been the pride and joy of the Navy, his very own flagship, and he was looking forward to showing her off. The captain was immediately imprisoned for negligence - though later released.

After many enthusiastic attempts over the centuries, the Vasa was finally raised to the surface on April 24th 1961, magnificent still - and almost completely intact.

She is permanently on display in the huge, purpose-built Vasa Museum, just a short distance from where she sank. 20 million people have been to see her already.

**

The poem on House Martins, I have entitled **House Martians** *partly because that was such a common spelling mistake amongst the children that I used to teach. Perhaps it will make them laugh - all these years later!*

***

Camel on Rails *recalls a happy chance meeting during the course of a cycle ride along the River Nile that I undertook for charity some years before.*

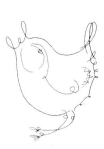